This Is Your Motivating Moment

Otishia Emmens

Otishia Emmens

The author has represented and warranted full ownership and/or legal right to publish all the materials in this book.
This Is Your Motivating Moment
Copyright © 2017 by Otishia Emmens
All rights reserved.
V.2
ISBN-13: 978-1975891329
ISBN-10:1975891325
Cover Photo-WallPapersCraft
Cover Design-Otishia Emmens
References:
African American Quotations, foreword by Jullian Bond, 2000

This book may not be reproduced, transmitted, or stored in whole or in part by any means, including graphic, electronic, or mechanical without the express written consent of the publisher except in the case of brief quotations embodied in critical articles and reviews.

DEDICATION

To all visionaries who refuse to follow the status quo, this book is for you. Stay religiously motivated.

Otishia Emmens

This Is Your Motivating Moment

Any Other Way

This is for those who would not have it any other way

For those who defeat, complete and fight, and for those who sit and get pissed but do absolutely nothing to ensure their life takes flight

This is for you go getter, legacy maker; changing the game for your family risk taker, for you complainer and you negative backbiting restrainer

I dare you to step off the cliff of excuses onto pillows of attempts and wrap yourself into the comforter of success….I DARE YOU!

Otishia "Ms. Tish" Emmens

Otishia Emmens

Foreword

What is your purpose? Your passion? Your destiny? Have you known for some time what you are meant to do for a career, but you just aren't sure how to transfer it to real life? Are you still searching for that path you can call your very own?

Some people spend lifetimes striving to reach their goals and dreams, which they believe, will one day make them happy. Yet many find themselves addicted to the pursuit of their vision, and the fantasy of what may come, instead of actually enjoying being happy.

When the understanding sinks in that your happiness is not based upon anything or anyone in the outer world, you start the journey towards being truly liberated.

This Is Your Motivating Moment is the story of such a journey. This book causes you to think, to smile and nod your head, yet it also faces and confronts some serious issues. It's a heaping helping of love, of sharing and caring by a woman who has experienced some of life's heartaches and rewards.

Empowerment and self-determination are two words that kept coming to my mind as I read this book. It's not just up lifting and informative, but a very necessary read. It speaks to the young and the old alike, through the author's honest ability to tie personal experiences of the past to relevant experiences of the present. She has given us the green light to go ahead and seek our best lives.

Kudos' to Ms. Emmens for having the courage and determination to speak up for those who can not or have not found their voice.

I am a firm believer that it is imperative you recognize what it is you're good at – what it is you really love to do, because your purpose in this lifetime is to do the thing that you love. Without your purpose identified firmly in your mind, you will wander through life, never quite feeling that you're "in" it.

I invite you to curl up in your favorite chair and get in

Otishia Emmens

touch with this author's journey, as she gets in touch with you. Each turn of the page is a wonderful step in the direction of your true self, and with every second you will discover that *"This Is Your Motivating Moment."*

Pat McLean

Director of TOMORROW'S GIRLS

Poet & Author

This Is Your Motivating Moment

Preface

Saying no and asking questions are things that I know and do best. The yes usually comes after I have weighed the pros and cons. At an early age, I have always been able to be consistent; even in my disobedience. If I liked or disliked something or someone, you knew it. The flood of emotions permeated through me intensely. It became my nemesis throughout my youth as I was not in a position to do anything about what I felt. It formed in my mind, cascaded through my facial expressions, controlled my body language and every now and again escaped passed my lips. Despite the discipline, it still did not stop me from being adamant about expressing myself. Was this my way of acting out or was my identity forcing itself to come out and meet the world? Most therapists would come to the conclusion that it was suppressed anger or in other scenarios a seasoned grandmother, aunt or uncle saying that I wanted attention. Whatever the diagnosis, I knew that I did not want the things that I was passionate about to go unrecognized. What has pushed me into the many successes in my life has been predicated on my motivation. Whether it was the things that I thought, read or witnessed in the atmospheres that surrounded me, the desire to want to change the events in my world gave me a uniqueness that was misunderstood by many but made clear in my mind.

There are individuals who seek accolades in order to ignite their aspirations and those who just till the ground until they find the right soil to plant seed. These individuals do not sit and watch for something to grow; they already know that something will produce from the seed. They move to more fertile ground to plant additional seeds and continue to do so throughout their journey in life. This is what I call the progressive nature of having motivation. When you accomplish a goal it does wonders for your self-esteem. You want to see what else you can do and how you will accomplish it. The rush of adrenaline that you feel propels you to heights never imagined. The way you look at things transforms into its own unique being. The sense of pride and ownership of your dream is realized not only to you but to those who become partakers of your hard work.

While staying motivated can produce feelings of glee, it is often the obstacles that tend to slow down your progress. It is not easy to see through the storms; frustration and discontentment are constant cheerleaders standing on the sidelines shouting out frequencies of doubt and reminding you of past failures. These elements can represent themselves in several ways. They are your friends, family, enemies, surroundings, money, resources and the most notorious of them all, you. We are our worst enemy when it comes to deciding whether to move forward with our ideas and sticking with "the plan." We provide fuel to our failures by allowing people and circumstances access to the blueprint of our goals. My grandmother used to always say to me that I talked too much; that my right hand should never know what my left hand is doing and that I curse myself when I give others the keys to the secret place. Listening to her preach mini sermons was not inviting however, once I began to experience the negative impacts, it quickly served as a valuable resource. When you invite others to hear your ideas, you create your own cheerleading squad. They will represent the team, wear the same uniform and rehearse the loudest chant but often times it fades into the background. You become bitter, hurt and angry because you do not see the support after a while. You are no longer the captain of your ship. You have lost the initial focal point of your motivation. The biggest fan should always be you and it should set the precedent for those who want to be on your team. There is another element to staying motivated, making sure that you have a solid foundation before you present it to others. People will always be star stuck by your ideas and level of dedication but they will never be able to give it the life you expect them to because they are not obligated nor should they be because it is your idea. We can avoid a lot of these traps by being committed to our ideas first and creating a firm momentum that does not shake its foundation when negative things threaten your vision.

Throughout this book the words idea, dream and vision will be exchanged. Many of you are at different stages of your life. As you read this book, the motivation you will need is going to vary in order for you to advance to the next level. Whether you are at the idea stage where the thought gives you a warm and fuzzy feeling, dreaming about the next step or have materialized your vision; all of it calls for the start and continued energy of staying motivated. Motivational levels range from expeditious to fighting to stay alive, in that order. When you give life to your idea, you are excited and the thoughts flood your mind like a tidal wave as you involve the elements of phone calls, marketing, opening up accounts, contracts and assistants. The excitement is lossed in the whirlwind of building. You are fighting to stay alive; trying to hold on to the thrill of that initial idea. It is during these stages that you find yourself asking "what did I get myself into" and you are tempted to put your well-meaning idea on the shelf because it just cost too much; it is taking up too much of your time and you could do it when you are more "stable and focused".

By now, you are shaking your head and probably saying "How did she know that?" Well, this book has been in the works for a while and I am a testament of what it means to religiously stay motivated. *From The Birth of The Idea to The Finished Product*, I have experienced countless pitfalls but as have I stated in the beginning (of this book), saying no and asking questions are what I do best and I want to share pieces of my journey on the road to my success along with some important tips to help you stay motivated and fulfill whatever brings your heart excitement and makes your world a better place.

In service,

Otishia "Ms. Tish" Emmens

Acknowledgements

I would like to thank my Lord and Savior, Jesus Christ. I can do nothing without your lead. I will never be ashamed to proclaim all that you have done for me. Thank you for giving me a life beyond my wildest dreams. You have given me revelation to the scripture, "The first shall be last and the last shall be first" **(Matthew 20:16 KJV)**.

To all of my mentees, I am so honored to be your mentor; I have nothing but the highest hopes for you. I want you to achieve past your failures and create a fabulous end to your stories!

To my staff and all of those who have given their time, I appreciate you more than you know. Thank you for putting up with my "monster" moments.

To my grandmother, the late Betty Emmens, your strength, honesty and sassy personality has been more than valuable, it kept my sanity.

To my mother, the late Deborah Mayfield-Emmens, your memory will always be lived and demonstrated through me. I will continue not to let the people "See me sweat."

To my sister, Ridshedia Emmens, you have been such a strong source of support. I pray that I have been a proper role model, big sister and friend.

To all of those who will purchase this book- Thank you. Now go do something with your life...LIVE IT!

FROM THE BIRTH OF AN IDEA...

Otishia Emmens

Chapter 1

Find Your Inspiration

Power Quote: "I Dare You to Step Off the Cliff of Excuses Onto Pillows of Attempts and Wrap Yourself In The Comforter of Success" Ms. Tish

It was 2006 and I was walking in a new direction that would change my life forever. One that would change the way I looked at how I would make a difference in the lives that looked to me for wisdom and encouragement. My life was going great. One of the top billing Litigation Paralegals in the law firm I worked; traveling all over the world and enjoying my circle of friends. I was offered the opportunity to become a facilitator over a girls mentoring program that served as an extension of community enrichment; co-partnered through the firm. For two years I conducted weekly workshops with young girls from various social and economic backgrounds, often pigeon-holed as "at risk" because of where the center was located. In a highly trafficked area of drugs and single parent households, I would pull up in my fancy car, step out in my business suit and enter into an atmosphere where my presence was not a frequent visitor unless it was for the purpose of capturing some media or corporate attention. I was not interested in either. I came to share the possibilities of having a future that would defy the odds. Welcomed with eyes of curiosity and uncertainty, I did not know that spending time with these young ladies would have such an impact on me. I quickly realized that all I had accomplish meant nothing if I was not giving back to my community. True satisfaction came from the ability to impact these young ladies in a way that would change how they looked at the realities of their world, culture and status in the neighborhood. The transformation became greater than I had imagined as I found myself having to go back to correct some wrongs in my life. I wanted to expand what I was doing because the need was too great to keep in one area. I wanted to break away from the tree and grow my own community development experience. This is where the inspiration came to launch TEworks and the challenge to stay motivated to explore the possibilities of change was presented.

Reality check: There is no straight way of maintaining

your motivation. It comes in various forms; in other words the noun is the same, but the verb is different. The positive side of motivation will keep you focused, reflective and non-judgmental. Learning to move with the pulse of your ideas and passions determines your pace. Oftentimes we are inspired by what we see and feel around us. Dancers are free when they dance, artist express their emotions with paint on a blank canvas. What inspires us the most will cause us to move. Inspiration breathes creativity and forces you to find the motivation to execute. To be inspired means to be awakened to the reality of your purpose. You develop your inspiration by surrounding yourself in atmospheres and around people who can keep that fire light. These elements are able to move you to discipline yourself to do things differently than what you were used to. Inspiration serves as a filter; you begin to prioritize what is important and what can be dismissed. It opens your eyes and your heart. Who would not want that? Only those who have made the choice to live with no hope; dismissing their purpose and aimlessly throwing away their gifts and talents. I am excited to know that this is not you because you are reading this book and that my friend has moved you one step closer. To what you ask? Well, keep reading to find out!

Chapter 2

They Will Claim You and Then Hang You

Power Quote: "Choose Your Friends and choose them well, but your business never tell for when your friends turn into foes, OUT IN THE STREET YOUR BUSINESS GOES" Unknown

Word began to spread like wildfire fast and soon people were looking to see what would become of TEworks. I spent much time sacrificing my personal life; dedicated to planning and building. I was happy and excited to bring a new dimension of services to communities where we were needed. Not thinking one iota that any negative responses would result, I made the official announcement. I stirred up some anger of taking the spotlight from a person who felt threatened by what I was doing. Soon enough, I was reading an email that made a serious but false statement that I was using the program I facilitated over to advance myself and the business. Nothing could be further from the truth. I thought to myself, "Wow, is this serious?" I received not only emails but passed on messages to ensure that it was made clear not to move forward. I could not believe it! Who would have a problem with something that was positive? Apparently it was the personality of one who thought they had me under their thumb; a personal puppet who as long as I did not raise my hand to speak, was all smiles and pats on the back. Using my creativity, passion and hard work to advance *themselves* was the motive all along. This was the first of many challenges that I faced and quickly introduced me to the harsh reality of doing business. A little shaken up, I began to call on my support group and we began to come up with a strategy to shut this foolish operation down. I had too much on my plate to accomplish and lives waiting to be changed. One suggestion was to confront the accuser face to face, or have a conference call that would include the officials of the program. The thought to do the later was tried. It turned out that the support that I had during my tenure with the girls program went quiet; no one spoke up to defend me. Despite all the good that I brought to the program, I just was not important enough to loose financial support over. It was done, the fighter in me came out and I was determined to send a message that any level of intimidation was not going to stop me from moving forward. One of my mentors said to me, "Otishia, I know you want to give them a piece of your mind but the best way to shut down a bully is simply not respond" "Oh, no honey!" with my hands on my hip, "My name is being slandered and lies are being told!" I wanted to show this person that I was not a punk. I found myself briefly moving away from my focus and had to pull myself together and really think. My mentor was right. If I gave any attention to the drama, I would be missing out on opportunities. It was too early for this to be happening. I decided to listen to the advice. One month after launching, I was invited to be on a panel of educators for a television show that aired in the tri-state region to speak on the power of mentoring. So many doors opened for TEworks after that show. The lesson learned from that experience was not to get mad but to get stronger.

Reality check: One minute you are cheered for your accomplishments and suddenly you become secretly envied and a threat. Who cares! Why waste your time and energy on careless behaviors from people who really do not matter? What is more important is that you remember the ultimate goal and that is finished what you have started. When you pay attention to the distractions, you get caught up in unnecessary drama that has nothing to do with your future. It is normal to

This Is Your Motivating Moment

have enemies, haters and vision blockers. Learn to expect the unexpected but do not give any of these characters life.

I would be lying if I said you do not need a support system in your corner; it is essential to your growth. Everyone wants to be supported; more so when you are feeling doubt about what you are doing. This is the best time to learn how to put self-discipline into practice. Having the ability to be reliant on the choices you make and being at peace with them secures a firm foundation to build upon. I tell many of our mentees to first create, execute and then expose. Keep your mouth shut until then and protect what is most important to you. The people who you allow to build you up will be the ones who will most likely not be around as you accomplish more. This is not a bad thing. As you achieve you grow; you desire to connect with those who look and think like you. If you are serious about the things you want advanced in your life you will become accustomed to adding and subtracting. Those who remain from the start are the ones who should benefit. Those who fall off, wish them well but do not try to figure out what happened. Keep your eyes and ears open because these will be the ones who will sell you out for a cheap buck because you do not give them as much attention or they see your life changing for the better. Never compromise your integrity because of a little pressure in fact; this should be the time when it shines through. Tell people "none of your business" or I guess I should be politically correct, "I cannot talk about it at this time" but you and I know that there will be times you will just have to tell somebody the former.

It is said; keep your friends close but your enemies closer. I would like to add, choose wisely. Sometimes it all runs too close and it is hard to tell who is who let alone the motive that lies behind the smiles, hugs and handshakes. A good way to discern is to allow the person to earn their space in your new life. Do not hand all the rewards of your labor on a silver platter. There are some things that should stay dear to your heart and other things you can afford to release at the appropriate time. If you understand from the beginning that people are not going to always see it your way then it will not startle you when the eyes shift, the heads turn and the mood swings seem to be more common than the music that play on your local radio station.

This Is Your Motivating Moment

But I Have The Scars To Prove It!

It was a rainy day and I had a presentation before an organization that provided services to children from despondent backgrounds. I just knew that once they heard what I had to say, I would be sure to land the contract to empower these kids. With my billboards, laptop and speech in tow, I proceeded to spill my guts and when I was done, I said to myself, "you did good girl." I looked at the faces around the table and as visions of success danced in my head I heard, "That was a nice presentation Ms. Emmens, but the kind of kids we have here, well your workshops will just not help them" What? Are you kidding me? I began to share why I was qualified to help. I shared some of my life struggles and the atmosphere changed. All of the sudden I became a welcomed part of the group. It just so happened that everything I worked on to present to these counselors was hindered because they were too busy looking at my outer appearance. They never heard me. The nerve!

Reality check #2: Never feel obligated to share personal struggles so that others can feel better about your success. I guess if I had come in that day busted, I would have been "relatable" to the kids.

This brings me to a very important tip for those who are looking to receive the golden award of acceptance from others. You will always become a puppet for the masses and you will lose yourself in a quick matter of time. People are going to talk anyway, so why make a big fuss out of trying to impress them? Set the tone for your life right now!

Your scars belong to you and no one else. They are the evidence of your survival; the ability to escape in just enough time before it turned into a wound. What we often do is show so much of our scars that we put ourselves in a position of venerability; we give others access to wound us all the more.

The battleground for achieving success is full of traps; be careful where you step and always evaluate the situation before you go in to fight. Sounds tiresome to always have to be on guard but life is a constant up and down roller coaster, but you determine how many times you will get on the same ride. People who keep circling back to dysfunctional habits will continue to attract manipulative mindsets that have no intentions of seeing you produce anything positive.

Chapter 3

Move Out The Way!

Power Quote: "There are people and circumstances already in line to provide criticism. You don't have to be the ring leader" Ms. Tish

I had to juggle all of it. I was still working as a Paralegal and squeezing in time to add pieces to my puzzle. I had to remove myself from everything that I knew. Being very aware that you cannot launch something with an old mindset, I had to move and think like a business woman. Never being one to stop something I have started, I will admit that I flirted with thoughts of quitting. Working sometimes sixteen hour days; prepping for a trial, dealing with opposing counsel and egocentric Paralegals who thought they owned the firm in addition to marketing my vision in between, I wanted to scream because I did not know which direction I was going in. I spent unnecessary money on marketing materials and burned way too much gas. I told myself that perhaps maybe I was way over my head and that no one was going to fully support my vision. I just had too much to do! Although opportunities were coming left and right, I did not feel totally confident. Do I take out a business loan to get a building or continue with bidding for contracts? This is when I realized I did not have structure. I recall meeting with a business advisor who had over 20 years' experience in the steel making industry and was now retired. He asked me "How is your mentoring business going to differ from the thousands of others that are out here?" I could not answer him immediately because I did not have that answer myself. I pondered on it and had an answer by our next meeting. Being asked that question forced me to think about all the pros and cons if I pursued a building or sat around and waited to be picked for a contract. TEworks was not given to me to destroy my life, but to change it for the better. In the end I decided that it would become a mentoring consulting firm where I could keep my boundaries open and not have to worry about overhead cost or the red tape that comes with bidding for contracts. I had everything I needed inside of me and I had to keep in mind that this was my vision and I was going to operate it the way I wanted. Once I settled with my decision, an ease came over me and it was clear that doing it my way would create a new way

This Is Your Motivating Moment

of how others would experience us. Today, we have conducted workshops in various states and continue to find new ways to expand our territory.

Reality check: I love to dance don't you? Instantly when I hear music I am singing, shaking my head and waving my hands. I immediately move outside of myself. I allow my true nature to come out in this mode. Of course when the music is off I am back to business and I move out of the way again for me to execute what needs to get done. Life will always be just like that; a constant shifting and changing of characteristics and frequencies. Know when it is time to get out of your own way and allow the best of you to come out. Nobody will ever know that you get nervous before you speak, scratch yourself profusely or eat a bag of chips before you go to bed. People see and hear what you give them. Wear your confidence proudly! Let it stand apart from all those insecurities that only seem to come out when you are in a public setting. Take it from me, when I am about to present to an audience, I am extremely nervous and often get anxiety however, the only person that knows this is me (and now you, shoot!). I tell myself that I am in control and that I have a job to do; somebody needs to be empowered and then I take a deep breath and go in for the kill. When you move out of your own way, you allow opportunities to flow unhindered and you will see just how valuable you are. People will seek you out for your expertise and respect what you have to give. Do not worry if all the accolades are genuine; you will be able to eventually decipher that. Transition into the type of person who has permanence! Who said you are not good enough? You need more material? You need more time? Only you will be able to determine how long it will take you to move from the pig pen into the palace. There are people waiting on you to lead them to a better way of living. Life is a cycle of networking, encouraging, correcting and giving. It can also be a place of closed doors, lost opportunities and empty promises. Get yourself out of the mud and at least try.

Never be your own worse critic. This is the kiss of death to any vision you are trying to build. Stop talking yourself out of opportunities that can set you up for stability. It is not fun to watch someone else fulfill their goals while you are still trying to figure out how to start your engine. We all have an innate power to fulfill what we daydream about; those things that make us smile, post pictures up in our work cubicles and on our refrigerators. The separator that prevent us from getting there is our constant disapproval of ourselves. If you spent just as much time investing into yourself; training, schooling, attending an empowerment workshop or simply finding a mentor (hint, hint) you will find that all of the fears are just an illusion. Step outside of those ugly thoughts for a minute and listen to what you are saying about yourself. How do you accomplish this? Ask someone else their honest opinion. Take it in and meditate on the comments and promise to work on your crazy self!

Reality check #2: Give yourself the license to produce; no matter how big or small the task is. Stop telling yourself that you messed up and now you have to deal with what you have. Positive thinking plays a huge role in the advancement of you. I find that many people have a short attention span in keeping a positive thought. Their lives are drenched with negative experiences that have impacted their lives in such a way that it totally incapacitates them. News flash! You are not the only one who has gone through debt, abuse, abandonment, low self-esteem etc. What distinguishes a winner from a loser is the fact that somewhere along the line there was a shift in how those negative experiences affected their lives. As a result, the winner turns their mindset into something that becomes a walking billboard for success and turns every evil thing said or done to them into a distant memory. How many green lights are in your lane? Put your mindset in "go" mode and drive it as far as it can; driving pass all the negative signs that have stood in your way for most of your life. Smugly look at your past and let it know that you will not be stopped from pursuing a life of peace and happiness. If you are bold enough, wear a badge on your heart and show it off every time you are reminded of all of your failures. Go ahead, I dare you!

Chapter 4

When People Can't Keep Up

Power Quote: "If you can't drink from this cup, then don't raise it to your lips" Ms. Tish

Working in a fast paced law firm environment taught me how to be quick on my feet and to always keep the facts in front of the faces of the attorneys. When specific documents needed to reviewed or produced before witness testimony at trial, all of the data gathered has to be complied into a spreadsheet, power point or binder readily available whether it was going to be looked at or not. There were times that a 200 plus request of witness binders had to be fulfilled yet they never were touched by the Judge. Either way, all of these steps called for precise communication with all involved; secretaries, vendors, in-house copy center, courier services etc. If there was one drop of the ball, off with your head! People lives and their money were at stake and the reputation of the attorneys and the firm weighed heavily as prospective associates looked to connect with top shelf firms. I transferred these same principals and work ethic into my business and was taking no prisoners. Those who could not keep up ultimately disappeared. One of my assistants asked, "Ms. Tish, when do you sleep?" "I only take cat naps" was my response. I knew that in order for me to be on top of my game, I had to stay twenty steps ahead of myself. That is what a good businessman does; keep his fingers on the pulse of his vision and never stops. The challenge was not being able to be consistent; it was being open to new ideas and revealing them to the ears and eyes it would hit. I did not want to be like everyone else; I did not want to have tea sessions or "Bleeding all over you" moments. I wanted to create a platform that would change the face of mentoring. Being the visionary and the face of TEworks would require elements that would stand out from the crowd. Yes, our workshops would touch on familiar topics but I wanted to be unique in how I presented them. I wanted to be committed to speaking truths that would make **people Find Their Talent and Work It Until Something Was Produced**. My personal favorite workshop conducted with our teens is "Interviewing-A New Approach." In this session we touch on the traditional skills that are used when going to an interview however, we also provide insight on how to take those same skills and incorporate them when meeting new people in social settings; more importantly when dating. Having options available to a young person's mind will make them more rounded and quick on their feet when dealing with the demands of peer pressure.

Reality check: When you find an avenue to funnel your ideas, walk it and show it off to all who will look and listen. Connect with the right vendors, radio stations and other public relations personnel who will be the promoters for your business. When you shop yourself around the same people and places they will grow tired of you. You want thirsty souls who have never experienced your services. You need staff that understand the importance of endurance and know how to carry out orders; minds that are evolving and passionate. Collect your staff from unusual places; college campuses, community leadership programs, from your neighborhood! Bring your creativity to the table and be bold in your presentation. So what if it's not the standard. Stand out and be the one who shines the brightest and rocks the loudest!

Throw Out the Nice Card

There is no room for being nice when you are running a business. You are going to be up against a plethora of mindsets and if you are going to gain the respect of those in the business community you must convey a seriousness that will ring clear when your name is mentioned. You do not have to agree with everything that is presented and you must always stay focused on the foundation of your business. If it has a similar ring to what you are doing; do not be quick to jump on the bandwagon. Check it out first; see if it compliments yours, if it does not, kindly reject it. Your name is on the line. Once you let an imposter in they can sabotage your vision and leave damage that you will spend years cleaning up. We see this in our government; when one president leaves, the newly elected has to come in and fix their mess before they can implement their own policies. This rule will be one of the most important building blocks to your business and life in general. Take ownership and never ask for permission to have a right to what belongs to you. Clients and business partners alike know my motto, "My time is very valuable and I won't let you waste it." I am consistent with this and need not speak it because it oozes through my actions, gestures and deeds. When I walk into a room I am about business. People should know that they can trust you, not how nice you are going to be. Time is money.

Chapter 5

Crossing Into Enemy Territory

Power Quote: "You must learn to turn your negatives into positives" Ms. Tish

"I am a damn good mother and I don't need anyone to mentor my daughter" screamed a mother who was very defensive as she witnessed her daughter achieving success in her personal life and in school. This young lady went from seeing herself as a statistic; having babies, being abused and drug addicted to defeating the odds. She received a scholarship to an Ivy League school and mentioned TEworks as playing a huge role in her achievements. We became the target of this parent and she was going to make it her business to let us know that it was she that gave birth and raised her. I looked at this insecure woman and had to let her know that what we did was an enhancement to what she was already getting at home (or should have been); that we were not interested in picking up any adoptive kids. The truth of the matter was that this young lady came to our workshops broken; tired from being in the middle of her mother's arguments and lack of discipline. Her mother was intimidated and did not know how to say thank you so instead she attacked. I experienced a few of these actions from parents; (mainly mothers) pulling their daughters out of our workshops, coming up with the silliest excuses to sitting in our workshops not to listen but to be disruptive because they had no discipline themselves. After having a few advisory meetings, I decided to launch a women's division. We would provide workshops that catered to women and the issues that affected them. It was evident that many of these women carried childhood hurts that spilled over into their adulthoods and needed to be mentored; to reclaim their self-worth. I launched the women's division and provided an outlet for women to be transparent with their hurts and insecurities. The mothers of these teens no longer had a reason to attack. Either they lined up or took their noise somewhere else. To date, our most popular workshop in our women's division is entitled Asset Recovery-Collecting Pieces of Me Again.

Reality check: Always have a clear and firm response

for those who want to attack what you are doing. Don't step down off your throne to tussle with court jesters. Shut down the operation before it gets started. Turn the negative into a positive and show your enemies a better way to get the job done. In most cases, they will become your most loyal supporters and you can use them to your advantage. This is not to imply being mean spirited, but learn to push your greatest enemies to the front when they want to cause trouble. Let them do the campaigning for you while you sit and collect on what is thought to damage your reputation. When the dust settles, you would have gained a new outlet to showcase your services and pick up additional clients/customers. Remember, *don't get mad, get stronger.* The best testing area to determine if you have something good is to bring it into this territory. Can your vision survive the threats, traps and disrespectful actions that it will be exposed to? Staying in a safe place will keep you stagnant. If you are trying to figure out why there are no sparks, ask yourself who have I started a fight with lately? Are you introducing your vision to atmospheres that will make you draw blood; make you fight back at any cost to claim your turf? It's a jungle out here alright, but if you are not ready, then stay in the tourist area where people will just look and never remember your name.

Chapter 6

You have to Pay to Play

Power Quote: "Own Your Life-Period" Ms. Tish

If there was one particular thing that would have told me that I could not build TEworks, it would have been the money factor. Looking at my budget every month; trying to maintain full control of where my money went was a balancing act. Nothing went out that did not represent me. The logo had to represent quality, class and finesse. Who was going to take me seriously if I printed out flyers on weak paper? If I conducted a teen workshop, I wore jeans but made sure that I still wore make up, my favorite bangles or earrings. I had to appeal to the crowd but at the same time not compromise who I was or the message I carried. Staff persons represented me and therefore the same rules applied; be yourself but remember you are representing a business. I poured that same energy into all of my marketing materials; making sure that everything went out on letterhead and business cards had to be of high quality. The website had to be bright, colorful and carry a message of success. I took all of my creativity and massaged it into my vision. If it did not work I did not put it out until I felt comfortable. It did not matter if I had one or three persons; my potential clients would never know. What was important is that the job gets done and our name is known. I asked a lot of questions and did research on how I could benefit from social media sites and did lots of observing; taking mental notes and bringing them back to the table to see if I could work around my budget; saving me time and money. Once I found out how beneficial these sites were, I was able to close out reoccurring accounts and put that money back in my pocket.

When the first teen conference was created, I was very stressed about where the money was going to come from. I did not want to have it at a recreational center; I wanted to give these young ladies an experience that had a mixture of familiarity and grand ambiance. I rented out one of the spaces at a hotel but wanted a menu that was fun. When I sat down with the events coordinator, I did not hesitate to lay out what I envisioned. I walked away with everything I wanted because I sent the message that TEworks was not just another mentoring project; we had lives to shift into high gear. Giving a very talented vendor the opportunity to create our materials, the event cards caught the attention of two major companies that filled our gift bags with free products. I never questioned my budget after that, if I wanted it I was going to get it because I found out that day that people will invest in quality and great presentation.

Reality check: Actions speak louder than words. If you say it then back it up with a message that will leave echoes in the ears of those who you want to support you. There will never be enough supply if you are always in demand. Activate those special skills to make up for what you do not have and watch the doors of excess open up for you.

Thank You for Your Invitation But...

During the first three years my fees were one third of what I charge today. My heart was so focused on giving back to the people that I walked on egg shells when the topic of pricing came up; yes, big mouth me! I wanted to be reasonable. However, as we began to expand, the needs became greater. I would spend most of my profit on gas and materials; leaving me with little evidence that I could show my accountant. I had to break free of this mindset and embrace my business as a fully operating one. If I spent my time investing in my presentations then I owed it to myself to get paid for it. At times it was overwhelming because I could not always afford to bring one of my assistants with me; I had to set up, break down and collect contact names, not giving me much time to focus. The financial burden was not one that would sustain me for long and I had to put into action a new plan. Putting a higher value on what I had to offer was going to be necessary for me to become more established. The years of being humble were behind me. I was in my fourth year of operating and it was time for me to see the fruits of my labor. Being concerned about whether people were going to pay the new fees for our services had to be removed from my mind. This meant moving into a different arena that would not second guess my quotes and had the backing to do so. What I had to offer was just as important as the popular mentoring organizations and I was not going to take on any more invites that did not pay what I deserved.

Reality check #2: When you are initially providing a service, you have to bend a little in order to get your product out there but keep in mind that recalculating your fees will ultimately become a factor. Do not expect for people who are not business oriented to understand this. Any successful company selling to the public will have to raise their rates in order to retain profitability. If you become mentally bombarded with the reactions of your revisions, you will never make any money. When you carve out a place for success you must be wise in how you maintain it. Not only does this include pricing and marketing, but turning away opportunities that do not support it. Get in the habit of saying no, no thank you and if you are bold enough, "absolutely not" Trust me, you will be respected in the long run for it.

Chapter 7

Control Your Stinkin Thinkin

Power Quote: "This is one of the glories of man, the inventiveness of the human mind and the human spirit; whenever life doesn't seem to give an answer, we create one" Lorraine Hansberry

Everything from my home, office, to the car I drive is the product of someone else and me having it adds to their success. I have never looked at anything and not wondered how well the visionary was doing in life because of the guts it took for them to step out and make it happen. To see the finished product of all their hard work must made them feel like a superstar. This is one of the motivating factors I keep close to my heart that keeps the drive in me to grow my business. Such power comes from extending a piece of you into the world. Everyday there is a chance to reveal a new invention and being aware of your God given talents adds to the excitement to turn it into something tangible! Giving back to my community; tirelessly speaking on various topics concerning individual enhancement, I found myself longing to go the extra distance to touch lives beyond my reach. While exploring networking ventures in California, I met with one of my business colleagues who introduced me to podcasting. This would allow me to reach a greater audience. Utilizing my time, I took some courses and later went into the studio to record my first session and was showed the ropes on how to navigate the recording software. When I got back to the East Coast, I was able to implement this into our services and soon after, launched our first podcast series entitled, This Is Your Motivating Moment. Within six months of launching, we acquired over 1,000 hits and were picked up by four podcasting sites that gave us more expansion. A sponsorship later followed. Our name is being introduced to people and companies that we would never be able to touch. Open doors and expanded opportunities came as a result of me telling my insecurities to shut up! I also found a new passion sitting behind that microphone. I was introduced to the fun and entertaining world of voice over acting. Having this opportunity to be the voice behind commercials, intros to radio shows, narrations for books etc. was totally unexpected. This was a gift for me to further advance myself and the business.

This Is Your Motivating Moment

Everything was relative; I could incorporate this into the business and add another component to our services in the future

Reality check: Ideas should not stay tucked away neatly in a pile. They are to be explored. Keeping a cap on them only hurts you. You have to dare to be different and stretch your mind beyond your capabilities. Your confidence will be a magnet to the right connections and will take you down the road of independence. Everything that surrounds your world is built from one's imagination and yours should push you into wanting to be a part of that revolution! Visionaries never launch something without mistakes and failures. Knowing that new discoveries will result from it will keep the fire light. If you find that you are hitting a brick wall, step away and give your mind some time to breathe; to rest only allows it to recharge and who knows what will develop when you do that! It is said that a mind is a terrible thing to waste, so are the discoveries that stem from it. If you have a love for something, it will find its way into your life somehow. Explore every inch of your hobbies. You never know where it can take you.

Chapter 8

Come Rain or Shine

Power Quote: *"We are all puppets in the hands of fate and seldom see the strings that move us"* Charles Chestnutt

During the years 2009-2010, everything got quiet all of a sudden. I lost contracts, calls stopped coming in and I found myself dancing with those nasty realities of being an entrepreneur. Was I doing something wrong? Why were the people not reaching out? Was my message getting boring? All of these questions were swimming around in my head yet, I still had to be on top of my game and operate as if none of it existed. Yearly business licenses had to be paid, social networking sites had to be updated and marketing our brand had to be done with quality. I was in a bind to nicely put it. How was I going to keep my head above water? I sat in my office, trying to figure out how to keep the strategic tips offered in our workshops alive in my own life; I was the one who invented them after all. What I did not realize was that I was going through a transition and in order to adjust, I had to move away from my current operations. What would benefit my firm in the beginning was not going to carry me for long. As the years went by, the needs became different and I had to keep up or else I would become just another mentoring program. Sitting in a quiet place was the best cure for what was a huge stomach ache to me. While I loved going back to the drawing board, I did it when things were thriving and I was adding to our services, but now it was totally different. I had to draw from my inner strength and let myself know that it was only for a season. Seeing no productivity, I had to learn the lesson of reinvention. When the workshops slowed down, I made up for it in other areas; podcasting, vending events, webinars, and conference calls. I had to keep the people engaged until the storm blew over. I knew that my vision was not in vain. I stayed in the ears of my mentees and followed up with contacts to let them know we were still open to sitting down and discussing new opportunities. With all of my efforts, I still did not receive any responses. After a few failed attempts, the light bulb went off; I had to keep the platform for TEworks so attractive that new business would come to us, not the other way around! When my perception changed, it opened my mind to a new venture (*Read chapter 18 to find out*).

Reality check: Change comes in the strangest ways and you can never know when it is going to hit you. Do not stop functioning because the tides of your plans shift. Building is supposed to include "elevator type" movements. Your control is heavily weighed by your behavior. When the hustle and the bustle of what you are doing slows down or comes to a complete stop, remember what your goals are. Instead of throwing up your hands, listen to the unusual sounds of change and take notice of the direction it is coming from. Determination is based on what you will do and what you will not accept. Do not be afraid to rearrange things, it is where new inventions are made, connections are created and new relationships are established.

Chapter 9

Everything Is Your Fault

Power Quote: "Never Complain, Never Explain"
Katharine Hepburn

Twenty five returned phone calls was made to apologize for the misrepresentation of a workshop that was put into the hands of another. I opened a new division and was excited to get it up and running. I had presenters and vendors ready to join forces to empower the women that would experience this event. One month before, instructions were sent out so that everyone was on the same page. The day of the event, I was confident that everyone knew their part and that it would be the least of my worries. Well, I was so wrong! The main presenter decided to go against what I wanted and waited to share it when the microphone was on (those things are dangerous in the hands of the wrong person). The look on some of the faces made me want to disappear yet at the same time jump up and holler "What in the hell are you doing?" Keeping my composure, I had to smile and kindly interrupt; following up with some quick back up plans to make my guests feel that their time was not wasted. I went into damage control mode afterwards. I found out later that the instructions were never read and the assumption was that it was a "free your mind" session. I could not blame anyone but myself. I did not think that I would have to spoon feed or hold the hands of an adult. Doing business with one that was familiar with me was a bad mistake. When I brought it to the attention of my advisory board, I was reprimanded for relaxing my standards and that it was indeed my fault for not securing someone who had more experience. There was no room for excuses because I knew that they were right. I let my heart get in the way and leaned too much on the novice and not the realist. I did find that something good came out of the experience. It revealed to me the lesson of truth and consequences. A true friend knows when to separate business from familiarity. When the two mingle, it leaves room for this testing ground to be addressed. I lost someone who I thought would be around for years to come. Who knew the aftermath would bring the friendship to an end. I was alright with that. I knew that whatever offense that could not be solved, did not need to be forced back alive. I never let anyone come that close to my business like that again. I learned that when something is that important to you, protect it at all cost.

Reality check: Be committed to being the brick layer. In order words, anything that is not rock solid should not go into your foundation; no matter how appealing it looks. When you try to force something abstract, it sticks out. An imposter always reveals himself at the wrong time to make you look like an idiot. This can be resolved by carefully evaluating whether or not it is beneficial to add the extra bells and whistles. When you think that people are looking for the grandiose, you will find that just being simple works best.

Reality check #2: In leadership, there is little room to blame others for mistakes that have your name on it; even if you were not the one who caused it. You are the face of your vision and everything that falls under it. If you become the type of person that depends on others to clean up your mess, you are headed for failure. Those who assist you along the way will quickly leave the mess behind if they feel the pressures of responsibilities they are not equipped to handle.

Remember, they are there to help you expand and grow; whether it is for a day, hours or years to come. Just because you have extra hands in place does not mean you put your feet up. Stay out in the trenches with them! This is how you will gain long standing support. Not being afraid to wear various hats will certainly strengthen your reputation as a good employer. Treat others with respect and watch your name/business blow up!

Chapter 10

Every Level of Power Comes With A Price

Power Quote: "Once you have danced, you always dance" Judith Jamison

I always had a "no holds barred" mindset. I knew that once I obtained the keys I could unlock any door I wanted. I just had one annoying problem, I had to wait, and wait some more. I sat on an education board for one year; watching countless amounts of money being passed across my eyes; it was distributing. I would always hear, "We need to bring something new and different into our districts" I would say to myself, "Duh, am I invisible?" The reality was that I was not an expert; I did not speak the language of the educators. I was there as an added incentive so there was not really much that could be done about funneling my business into the scope of their curriculum. A place had to be created for me. For one year I listened, smiled and networked without trying to seem anxious, not realizing that I was being prepped for a certain level of power. All the thoughts of me being made to wait were not the case at all. If I was given the authority to head some of the workshops too early it would have been too much for me to handle. Even though I brought a level of power and expertise to the table, a premature move would have damaged my name and a future relationship with the board. I was in the right position to be developed; to learn the intricate nature of the educational system. This could only enhance what I would bring once the keys were placed in my hands. When the time came, I landed two state contracts and established a place for TEworks within the school district. We further went on to work with other programs sponsored through the district that focused on strengthening parent-child relationships. Being a part of this growth established us as a vital part of this community.

Reality check: Like a game of chess, the right move will allow you to "king" your opponent. Every calculated move must demonstrate a level of expertise or else you will be bounced back to square one. Slow and steady wins the race. Win big by learning what the red, yellow and green symbols mean when working with other organizations. Respect the order of other

This Is Your Motivating Moment

businesses and you will always have an invite to come and play. A good player does not force himself on anyone. He waits, but knows how to keep his target steady until he is ready to hit the mark.

Otishia Emmens

...TO THE FINISHED PRODUCT

This Is Your Motivating Moment

Otishia Emmens

Chapter 11

Leaving The Past Behind for Better Business

Power Quote: "The best lessons, the best sermons are those that are lived" Yolanda King

Most, if not all of the workshops conducted represent my life. When I started the business, I made a vow that I would never stand in front of people to deliver something that I had not mastered. I noticed that people gravitated to what they knew and more importantly, wanted to be inspired about how to get through. With every word spoken, I brought healing to myself concerning painful topics of my childhood and experiences as an adult. To my surprise the tips provided were never heard of in certain atmospheres. It left me puzzled because topics such as feminine hygiene, safe sex practices and education were not discussed in a lot of households. It made me very aware of how I was raised; picking and choosing what to address; what to let fester and ultimately bury itself only to rear its ugly head trying to kill my self-esteem when I experienced disappointment. I remember sitting in my bedroom one evening and I had this overwhelming sense of anger that came out of nowhere (so I thought) I must have cried for at least two hours and could not figure out why. Over the course of three years, I felt the need to confront a family member concerning some missing pieces of my life. Things that were allowed to take residence that should have keep me protected. Questions like why I was uprooted from the city I was born (Philadelphia) to being forced into a new family structure I absolutely hated. Never one word being mentioned about my deceased mother, down to a sister and brother along with other family members that were kept away from me. All of this played a huge role in who I was and how I reacted when certain topics were mentioned. Rejection, abandonment, physical and emotional abuse were all elements of my world growing up. I experienced some of these things and witnessed others. It kept me in a very angry place for a long time because I felt slighted from having a normal life; I could not be a kid. I had to grow up fast. I learned how to wear a mask well; how to smile and even "pray things away" without honestly dealing with them. This was not who I wanted to be. It simply was not me. I never got to see the real me until I dealt with the seeds that were planted by others. I could not present anymore workshops or private mentoring sessions until I severed myself from my past. This was how I chose to do it; keep it real, no matter how ugly it was. I desperately needed balance so I could be the best me and more importantly present a better business model. Every day I strive to live in my freedom; away from the experiences that have tried to taint me. TEworks is my life and I am thankful that I have been given the task to shape the fragile minds of our youth and women. I am proud to be able to look someone in the eye and tell them the truth about myself and challenge them to do better. I wanted to do a serious kind of business and I had to start with me.

Reality check: There is no way you can fully separate your business from your personal life. Every intricate detail compliments or spoils the other. If you think you will be able to do business all the time, you will ruin other qualities of who you are. Because we are multi-faceted beings, we have to be able to bring a neutral ground to our lives. You cannot be family oriented and not spend time with them because you are running a business. The start of businesses, ideas, visions etc. is the result of our personal lives. Growing up in a family of singers will impact you in a way that you may want to be in the entertainment industry. Working in a family owned store or company will trigger an entrepreneur component in your decision making in life. The realities of these humble beginnings help to shape us into who we are. When our lives are jolted by bad experiences, we must look at them, see where it went wrong and commit to fixing the problem if you want to be an excellent representation to what you are giving to the world. This should be the heart and soul that drives you to success.

Otishia Emmens

Chapter 12

Rules of Leadership

Power Quote: "Whatever you do, do like a church steeple: aim high and go straight." Rudolph Fischer

I never stop, whether I am at the mountain top or in the worst of valleys, I never, ever stop. My mindset is to always at least try, go back to the drawing board or take a short rest, only to dive back in again. There is not one person connected to me that can refute that. I have been a leader from the womb and knowing that has made me an invincible force. Anything that I have wanted, I have been able to accomplish. I put myself through college, built a twenty-years plus legal career, traveled, owned property and drove what I wanted. Launching TEworks was inevitable. I refused to believe that a 9 to 5 job was the total supplement to my survival! I have too much zeal not to become my own brand. Daily, I focus on working every gift inside of me to finalize how I would own the rest of my life. I wholeheartedly believe what my God says about me and I do not make any excuses for it at all. I am truly blessed. My ability to lead did not always come by way of opening up my mouth. I was a very timid little girl however; my actions always shined through my hard work and discipline. As I gained confidence, I detached myself from being content with the world's demands and restrictions. My boldness to dare to be different has often times kept me in a place of isolation; only to refine me. Being comfortable with being by myself has been puzzling to others. I believe that when you have a lot of people surrounding you, confusion is always at your hip. I have been a loner all of my life; only inviting those who are worthy of my presence. Sounds cocky, but when you think about it, there are some people who do not have this luxury. Their lives are always bombarded by others. I hear a lot of my business colleagues speak of never having any time for themselves. I cannot imagine not having that option. You have to be "selfish with your time and make people respect that" is what I always say. I find these same principals to hold true in running my business. Because I hold my peace of mind, friends and family at a high standard, it is easy for me to stop what I am doing. I learned early in the start of this vision not to mix business with pleasure; nothing good can come out of it. Forgetting how to live; enjoying the simple things in life can chip away at your integrity and cheapen your self-worth. When I speak, I do it with experience, passion and a captivating spirit. Walking the walk and talking the talk is more important to me than being popular. The greatest spotlight is the one that closes the show. I know how to do that well. These are some of the good qualities that have come as a result of me keeping the scales balanced. Possessing these types of leadership skills has given me a life where I keep myself in the position of being able to choose and I love every moment of it.

Reality check: Rules are made for a reason. Becoming a strong leader is one of the benefits. Here are some standard rules I live by:

1. Show up on time (I like to arrive 30 minutes early).

2. Remain consistent, even if you are having a frustrating day.

3. Be confident. Take pride in your vision.

This Is Your Motivating Moment

4. Manage your time. No means no and yes means it can be accomplished.

5. Stay creative and find ways to expand.

6. A good name should put a smile on the face that mentions it.

7. Have patience, knowing that everything will fall into place.

8. Be extremely selective.

9. Smile at the fools who do not take you seriously.

10. Have class and integrity at all times.

Otishia Emmens

Chapter 13

Practice the Art of Staying Free

Power Quote: "A man is free when he sees himself for what he is and not as others define him" James Cone

Every once in a while I come across someone who thinks like I do. It is like finding a rare jewel; you want to show it off but then again, you want to be selfish and not spoil it with exposure. These individuals are my close friends and family members that I value so much. They are the confidants that I can count on when I am having challenging moments. I find freedom in who I am and not what I am expected to be when I am in their presence. Proud of my accomplishments, I am never envied or judged. If I am acting out of character, I am told immediately and for that I am humbled to have them in my life (because I can be a monster sometimes). Enhancing others with empowerment and giving back to my community can be a daunting task. To be able to come back to a place that is familiar is always needed and I have that not only within myself but in my surroundings. This is how I stay free. I make it a top priority that no matter how much I obtain that I can always look back and see my support. I choose my environments; not the other way around and I do not bend on my values. I have accepted the truth about those who have dismissed themselves out of my life and those whom I had to release. I was once told that I was a follower and I would never succeed in life. Well, I would like to tell that person, you got it wrong, so very wrong. Not only have I excelled, but I have soared to a place of stability that they will never obtain because of their negativity. In fact, I would like to take this time to thank all the persons who thought I was never good, popular, smart, important or ambitious enough to fit into their world. You were right, how could all of this fabulousness possibly fit?

Reality check: We stay stagnant because of the words and actions of others. It becomes a piece of jewelry we wear and every time we think we can do better, we take one look at it and surrender to its trance. If you think about it, freedom does not follow you around asking to be your best friend however, negativity and bondage does. Freedom waits for you to come to it.

What are you waiting for? If there is a chance that you can eliminate half of the baggage that is keeping you in tight corners, why not at least give yourself enough respect to at least reach out and grab that piece of light that is peeping through your dungeon. There are a lot of arrows pointing to freedom and guides that will help you along the way. Where you do not see either; you need to run like hell!

Beware of the Word "They"

"They" said that you are way over your head, "They" said you should do it this way, "They" said that you are not giving enough of yourself, "They" said you think you are better. When I asked my assistant who was "they" she could not answer me. I told her that I was going to charge her every time that word was mentioned. Worrying about what others have to say about me does not exist when I am working to complete a project or present a new one. That term and whoever was attached to it did not come home with me when I was tired yet, had to finish writing out a proposal, did not help me to budget money so I could run both my household and business, did not go with me when I had to get sponsorships and does not have a heaven or hell to put me in. Ignoring the "they club" is another way I practice the art of staying free; I chew the meat and spit out the bones as my grandmother taught me. There have been some people who have helped me along the way that now see the fruits of my labor and secretly have tried to peg me in the space of where I started with their passive aggressive tactics. Even in the most confusing times did I ever have the mindset that I was out of bounds with the direction of my life. I was not sure why things moved so slowly but I made sure that I did not lay my baton down. I kept it in my hands and ran into the arms of my freedom!

Reality check #2: This word ("they") can become a heavy hitter in your mind if you allow it. No one will fully understand what it takes to make your dream a reality. Pushing through the crowd of uncertainty will take a lot of mental and physical muscle. Adding busy bodies to the mix will only create more work for you. Welcome advice that only compliments your goals and be quick to close off the pipeline of quicksand comments that leave you motionless. Remember, what you digest is going to come out in your actions. If this is the case, let it be something rock solid.

Otishia Emmens

Chapter 14

Make Your Announcement

Power Quote: "I believe that I was born to help my people to be free" Muhammad Ali

I am Black and I am a woman. I celebrate that. I am proud of my history and the contribution it has made to this country. I never back down from uncomfortable topics regarding my people. I will always have a great love for my community; this is why I designed TEworks. I wanted to build a bridge that would service needs that are most important; family, education and cultural awareness. The social and economic lack can be addressed swiftly by speaking into the ears of our youth values that will catapult them into arenas unknown or rarely focused on. Parents can benefit from having information on where the best tutor programs and schools are located. Sitting and talking about options that would trigger a different point of view is the heartbeat of my vision. In our Black communities we have a plethora of bright, creative minds waiting to be watered and discovered. The journey of my career has led me to this very thing, to bring knowledge back of what can become of your life if only you apply yourself. This is the common thread that is communicated in our workshops. Knowledge is power and having it in numbers strengthens the cord. On that note, I would like to say that whatever negative images that are projected in the media about our children; be mindful that for every stereotype there is one who will challenge it. All Black children are not dysfunctional or destructive. They have the type of potential that can extend far beyond "the hood". I salute every involved parent that invest and nurture their seed, who take the time to raise their children with the knowledge of what makes them different, yet special. It is because of your motivation that Black leaders are representing nations and teaching other cultures the truth about the richness that flows from our ancestors.

Reality check: You have a voice and the ability to use it for community development and it is welcomed by those who are waiting to listen. Who are you? What needs are being met? Are you networking outside of your homes? Where are you taking your message?

How far is it reaching? Questions like this should be at the front of your mind when pursuing your vision, dream, purpose and destiny. There is only one you and nobody can duplicate it. Make your stamp on this world with all that fire bubbling inside of you! Exhaust everything you are supposed to. Your announcement should make others take notice and build upon what you have established. This is the power of innovation and the benefits of leaving behind a legacy.

This Is Your Motivating Moment

Chapter 15

While You Were Laughing

Power Quote: "You see things and you say, "Why" But I dream things that never were; and I say, "Why not" George Bernard Shaw

The timeline of my life has been flooded with these types of journeys; going to school with no money, looking for my first home with no money, going into the dealership with no money but driving out of it with a smile on my face to quitting a very stable job to pursue my dreams. I would like to tell you that everything I have received has been because of my faith and that would be part true. More so it was my determination to make my enemies look like fools. I never doubted my capabilities, but there were many who did. The gossip topic with my name headlining it was the norm for many years. Am I mad? Not anymore but, there was a time honey that I just wanted to fight and curse out people. I had such a great disdain for the "peanut gallery" especially at the church I attended. I felt like no one understood me and that was very heart bending. In an atmosphere where there should have been strength and support, there was not much, but because of the greatness in me I got accustomed to it; being called crazy to being too radical. I understood after while that this was a set up for me to push until I broke through the walls of ignorance. All great minds; no matter what race or gender has endured these reactions from their so called "dream killers". What was not evident to the eyes that judged were the jewels that only I had access to. There was a declaration spoken over me as a little girl that I was going to become someone great. I hid that in my heart for years. At the sound of those words, I became tattooed once my mother spoke it. I remember feeling a jolt go through me when I heard them. I thought she meant that I was going to a big superstar. Too immature to understand, my head got big. Now, being famous was not ruled out as an option however, I did not know at the time there would be some grooming and numerous obstacles to conquer before I stood in that position. Passionate not to become what I saw around me I worked hard; fears sweat and tears. The quote that you often see under my logo; "Find Your Talent and Work It Until Something Is Produced" is my theme. While many were trying to give me the antidote to my "issues" I would sit quietly and chuckle on the inside saying, "Well, we will see about that". A "thank you" or a simple smirk would come across my face because my life was already marked to succeed. I could sleep at night because any mistakes made along the way could not create a cloud dark enough to cover my shining light. I tell my mentees, when you enter a room, people will see the essence of who you are by the energy you bring to it. You never have to say a word. Just enter in and you will attract what you need.

Reality check: Be brave! Do not let your heart get smashed by empty words. Remember what it is that makes you smile. Those that choose to work in private will always draw attention to themselves. It makes others curious about you. Where there is no information, people will choose their ammunition. Personalities in the public eye are scrutinized because of what tabloids create about them. Some choose to ignore it and others spend lots of money trying to make them go away. If there are ponds filled with piranhas do not step in them! Push those who oppose you in it by succeeding!

Otishia Emmens

Did You Forget?

There had been some very hard times endured because of my commitment to make my dreams a reality. Some so heart wrenching that I never stopped to think about all the seeds of inspiration planted in me. Never one to write things down, I had conditioned myself to only remember what I wanted. I began to tag things that took me back to certain words and deeds. From there, I would develop a strategy to pull myself out of situations that threatened my future; whatever or whoever told me no, I reminded myself of why I deserved it (I was going to become someone great). Low self-esteem, self-doubt nor a defeated spirit was no match for that! I often wondered why everything had to be so deep, so mysterious and to be quite frank with you, fucking difficult! It hit me one day that it was in these trying times; I climbed the highest, fought the hardest and demanded the most. People would scratch their heads and I am sure were thankful that it was not them. I would look back and say, "You're lucky it's not you". Those times of revelation for me changed how I perceived my hard places and shaped my individuality. I was always one to go against the grain; adapting to the phrase "Grace Under Fire" did not take long. I quickly became immune to life's blows; it has made me strong as an ox. I proudly say that my strength is my most beloved trait. When I mentor, I mean business; I am not sympathetic to whiners or lazy persons. I will not accept from any of my mentees defeat. I push them because I have been down the road of hardships and losses. My approach is hard driven, yet simple. You decide whether or not you will choose success or failure in your life.

Reality check #2: When you are going through some tattered experiences; it will make you crossed-eyed at what has become of your life. Pull from your inner self. Try something new for a change. Seek out some positivity! Choose to remember the fun times you had before you became so inundated with responsibilities. Walk down a different path; pull out your favorite book; it may trigger a nostalgic emotion, turn on your favorite song and listen carefully to the words. Share some laughs with family and friends. Let the truth be known of why you are who you are. Self-affirmations in the mirror are the best medicine to help you not forget that you are alive. Making the best out of each and every day when you do not feel like it will transform into a discipline. Teach someone a valuable lesson by sharing a little piece of you. A kind word or deed will help you to remember!

Chapter 16

Are You Having Any Fun?

Power Quote: "The question isn't who is going to let me; it's who is going to stop me" Ayn Rand

I am having the best time living and learning along the way. I rarely regret what I say or do. I celebrate that; being able to be honest with myself and those around me. It is part of my charm, my wit and needed when I am sending a serious message. I always leave something on the table for thought; for inspiration. I love to laugh and be silly and I bring these elements into the workshops. I am a realist; my words will cut to the bone and make you angry yet, at the same time you will respect me for it in the end and want to come back for more. In my opinion, many have lost the hunger to stand out and let the real "them" shine. I am Otishia "Ms. Tish" Emmens and I am proud of it! I was not always this way though. I never wanted to be around crowds or open up to unfamiliar faces.

This Is Your Motivating Moment

Tensions between me and my destiny were always at battle. Operating TEworks has been one of the strongest lifelines I could ever ask for. While I still am not a social butterfly; I no longer hide my gift from others. When I found my voice I never stopped talking. I guess spending all those years watching and listening gave me much content for what I am doing today. My favorite observation of others is seeing them advance from one level to the next. When you can play a role in helping others achieve their success, it makes you feel good. The deed boomerangs and allows you to grow and expand the vision you have for your life. I never want to be selfish in anything that I do; cemented doors are not fun to pry open. If I give it then I know the doors of "yes" will be available for me to walk through.

Reality check: Teach yourself to love and appreciate what you have to offer to this world and have fun doing it. Everything does not call for a rigid presentation. Turn off the prohibit lights and have some fun! There is a time for everything to have its proper moment. When you show others a side of you that is normally unknown, you are providing a balance to all the components of what you represent. Too much of anything becomes monotonous to those who are on the receiving end. Shake it up a little; provide some variety to keep yourself from getting bored and eventually uninterested in your gift. Savor those moments that made you proud to be unique and special. Show what you got!

What Happened To Our Personalities?

It took me some time to get to a place where I was completely comfortable with myself. Never one to overdo it, I always strive to make calculated moves. My ability to stay the course until completion is very much part of my personality. Call it what you want; stubborn, corny or difficult, it has reaped me a copious amount of rewards. With so many distractions serenading me on a daily basis, I have made a commitment not be an empty shell that others can just pour their toxins into. If I have to dismiss you for a long period or forever, I do not have a problem with it. I will not let anyone get in the way of what I have to do. This is the serious part of me. This is the tag I am known for. Am I in the popular crowd because of it? It depends on who I am in front of. Sometimes, I give all sides of me and there are times when I am one dimensional for the purpose of carrying out my assignment; but I guarantee no matter which side you get, you will not have to question whether you will be entertained.

Reality check: The strengths of your character will bring exposure to your personality. When you are born to do great things, you have to utilize every ounce of charisma in you. Being afraid of who you are will not serve you well when it is time to put your plan into action. If the shoe was on the other foot, would you want someone to give you half of who they are? When you do not like or are afraid of yourself, it will show in everything you do. This is not a good recipe for staying motivated. If you do not know who you really are, pay attention to those trigger points in your attitude and behavior. Take note of them and bring balance however, never, ever expect others to understand you until you can get a handle of what makes you tick!

Otishia Emmens

Chapter 17

Going Green

Power Quote: "If you have but one wish, let it be for an idea" Percy Sutton

I thought long and hard about the logo that would represent TEworks. I wanted something that represented growth, strength and solidarity. What would be displayed in our workshops had to capture not only the eyes but the heart. I came up with a tree. I am captivated by its ability to make a statement whether it stands alone, amongst others or adds to the beauty of our surroundings (homes, parks, woods etc.). I thought about the versatility that it provides and produce; fruit for us to eat, furniture for us to sit and lay in, paper for us to write on. I wanted all of these elements to be streamlined into my vision. I specifically choose the oak tree because it has longevity and can withstand the most unyielding climates. The roots of this tree run deep and cannot be easily destroyed. I do not know of a better comparison to my life. Nothing else spoke to the twists and turns of events that would bring me to the moment of launching my own business. The name (TEworks) is a big entity; bright, thirsty for expansion and standing strong. We offer a variety of services (group workshops or private mentoring) that cater to the needs of the group, individual or small business. Our mentees come from various backgrounds, all contributing to the diversity of the business. Our mission is to provide life skills mentoring workshops for the advancement of healthy lifestyles. The foundation of being successful is to have stability to handle all aspects of life. Workshops that provide "in your face" challenges and strategies that will assist with helping to navigate through life experiences particularly, conquering fears that hold you back from your destiny. Results that produce "good fruit" in your life so that you are empowered to give back to your community. That is what lies in this logo!

Reality check: What defines you? Find something that speaks to the message that you carry. It should be an applicable one that stands out in a crowd or can be a shining star by itself. What can you provide to those who come across your path? Will it be worth the exploration? It is said that when your life is over; you want to leave a legacy that others will want to follow. While that may be true, you want to have the influence while you are alive. Restore those broken pieces one success brick at a time. Your brand will speak for you at the point of acknowledgement. Find access to the places and people who will want to glean from your experiences. Why hold back or drown out the specialties of your life? If you are going to be a slave to something, make sure you are getting something out of it. Use your name/brand to give and it shall be given back to you with good measure.

Chapter 18

What I Thought I Knew

Power Quote: "Human dignity is more precious than prestige" Claude McKay

I thought I would be at the top of my game in the legal world, I thought I would have Esquire behind my name. I thought I would retire with credentials that would stop the presses. I thought I would be able to juggle both a small business and my legal career. Not! I had to give up one and had to be at peace with doing it. I sat in my office one day looking at the four walls and said, "Is this really what you want?" I had worked so hard at obtaining my degrees and building my career. I had convinced myself that I would wait for the perfect opportunity to come my way and then I could walk away from the corporate world however, everyday became more frustrating coming into an atmosphere with the knowledge that I was growing someone else's vision and not getting the credit I fully deserved. I could not live with the fact that I did not take the plunge to run my business full time. So, I jumped; faith first and fears behind me. After years of building, reinventing and stumbling, I owed it to myself to have the final say over my life. I gave up the steady paycheck, business suit, blackberry and trial preparations in exchange for entrepreneurship. I was not sure how I was going to be able to handle all the details but I knew I did the right thing because I was able to exhale. With more time on my hands; I took advantage of the entities that TEworks is associated with; the Small Business Administration and the Women Business Enterprise and began to look for more expansion with a greater influence. What I had accomplished within five years had to take on greater meaning. One thing I always wanted to do was explore opportunities in the global market. I networked with foreign exchange agencies to make this a reality. I applied myself in the same way I always had; made my presence known until I got results. I took the initiative to put myself out there; bare-faced, not knowing anything about exporting. I let my passion be the driving force and I am proud to say that TEworks is on its way to hosting services in other countries and the Caribbean islands. Providing tools for the advancement of healthy lifestyles, bringing our mentees in close contact with other mentees, we are bridging the gap between worlds far apart. International influence baby!

Reality check: Have you been feeling the pinch of reality closing in? Take heed to the pressure and do what your life is begging you for. Turn it loose! The greatest pleasures are found in exploring the "what if's" and adhering to your own rules. You never know what you will find on the other side of that mountain. Keep climbing and exploring. Throw out that rope, you will be surprise who will take hold and pull you through!

Otishia Emmens

Chapter 19

My Reality Check

Power Quote: "I had a way of life inside me and I wanted it with a want that was twisting me" Zora Neale Hurston

I want to let you in on a little secret. TEworks saved me from a life of triviality. I have found my true passion; being a pacesetter. Every traumatic experience helped shape my truths for a great work. Whether I am standing before a crowd, sitting face to face with a broken soul or speaking to hundreds through my podcast, I am collecting pieces of myself and recycling these lessons back into the world. I truly love what I do now. I understand what my name means and the depth of responsibility it carries. For years I never felt comfortable with my name; I went by the abbreviated version (Tish). That does not fly now; you need permission to nickname me. I am in touch with the value that it carries and I will not cheapen the creativity that my parents put into my introduction. **(T)**ish **(E)**mmens **(W)**orks has unlocked so many mysteries concerning myself. I have learned what it means to go after my destiny. I have learned what gives me the most joy and what gives me pause. I like my honesty and the uniqueness that it carries. I like to challenge myself to destroy the stereotypes of Black women. I am passionate about my culture; the sacrifices made for me were nothing short of astonishing. I have explored the depths of my drive. When I hear the words, "You can do whatever you put your mind to" I am driven enough to believe it. I have felt the pain of rejection and abandonment as a result of confronting the ugly realities of my life and those who have played their roles. I have added great triumphs and erased years of lies. This is what exploring that tiny seed of inspiration has done for me. I never would have given myself enough attention to all of these things had I not moved out of my own way. I listened to the echoes of voices telling me who I was (or was not) and I built my own land and now I am dancing on it! "I am a positive image in my community, my actions represent how I view myself and the impact it has on my peers. I celebrate who I am and the accomplishments I have made thus far. I am a positive image and I represent the world." This vision statement is the mandate on my life; it is my

Otishia Emmens

lifeline when I am feeling unraveled and misunderstood. It is my remedy. I choose to live life with purpose and on my terms. I have come full circle and I will continue to play every note that this life is sending my way.

Chapter 20

I Dare You

Power Quote: "In one hand you have a dream, and in the other you have an obstacle. Tell me, which one grabs your attention? Henry Parks

I want to talk to you, yes the person who is reading this chapter right now. I know it is scary to step into the unknown, but that is what life is about. You know what you have dreamed about, what keeps disturbing your sleep; what keeps you day dreaming. Not having all the answers is not a good enough reason to drag your feet. Sometimes the answers come when you take the first few steps. There is something to be said about one who is brave. They are able to cross boundaries that embark them on a journey that leads to their financial, spiritual and mental freedom. When I decided to give myself the opportunity to soar, my life became a beautiful place. I want this for your life. How beautiful can an atmosphere that makes demands on your life be; always taking, never giving you any time for your purpose? What fun is spending a lifetime listening and watching other people's success? It is easier not to try than to be the catalyst for change. To create a legacy is so important. I am daring you to re-establish yourself. Learn to listen, be an example to those who will come after you and get the very best squeeze out of everything you want. Step outside of your territory so others can connect with you. Many of life's hidden treasures are beyond your backyard. How much value do you place on yourself? Are you a cheap dollar bill or are you that rare gold coin that is sought after? It is the unconventional moves that create the most powerful testimonies.

As you read about my journey to entrepreneurship, my goal was not to have you focus on me owning and operating my business. It was to get you to understand what is connected to your destiny when you decide to walk in it. Money, time, and popularity are the benefits. Being able to see the true essence of who you are is worth more than the above mentioned. For me, this experience has exposed my self-worth. I realized that for years I operated under a false sense of who I was. I spent years chasing after something that would not give my soul gratification. You cannot get back the time lost however; you can spend the rest of your life setting milestones. I want your life to read something like this: "I once was lost, but now I am found". This powerful affirmation can read as a road map to where you want to be in your life. Of course I want you to be at the "Found" part of that statement, but finding yourself is the task, and I am not speaking on just the emotional component of your being. I am speaking on your entire life. So think about where you want to find yourself before your journey ends. Yes, that is the scary part of it all. You do not know when that will be; my point, find it now and live!

Otishia Emmens

Power Quotes

"One does not fight to influence change and then leave the change to someone else to bring about." **Stokely Carmichael**

"The paradox in life is that one must be ambitious to be free from that ambition which corrupts and blinds and tempts and distorts." **Peter J. Gomes**

"Strangely enough, I can never be what I ought to be until you are what you ought to be." **Martin Luther King Jr.**

"The realization of ignorance is the first act of knowing." **Jean Toomer**

"Leadership means everything-pain, blood death." **Marcus Garvey**

This Is Your Motivating Moment

"Life for me ain't been no crystal stair." **Langston Hughes**

"Mistakes are a fact of life/ It is the response to the error that counts." **Nikki Giovanni**

"Never shirk one simple duty: Earn your honors, earn your rest." **Walter H. Brooks**

"Failure to recognize possibilities is the most dangerous and common mistake one can make." **Mae Jemison**

"You may know my name but, you don't know me." **Betty Emmens**

"None of us are responsible for our birth. Our responsibility is the use we make of life." **Joshua Henry Jones**

Otishia Emmens

"If you don't have confidence, you'll always find a way not to win." **Carl Lewis**

"When you want to do something in life, you have to focus." **Roslyn McMillan**

All quotations in this book are from Richard Newman, foreword by Jullian Bond, "African American Quotations," foreword by Jullian Bond, 2000.

This Is Your Motivating Moment

ABOUT THE AUTHOR

Otishia "Ms. Tish" Emmens uses her gifts to transform lives. A dynamic speaker, motivator and encourager, she has the ability to leave you empowered and fired up to fulfill your purpose! Her motto is "Find Your Talent and Work It Until Something Is Produced." When she is not writing, Ms. Emmens is an advocate for parent-child relationships. The Founder and CEO of TEworks Mentors, she provides life skills training workshops to various organizations, churches and businesses that have programs geared towards healthy lifestyle living. Her passion for mentoring derives from her own childhood experiences and cultural history. Her raw, direct approach challenges her mentees to take responsibility; to live in a victorious state of consciousness. The host of a podcast, This Is Your Motivating Moment, she empowers listeners all around the world.

Carving out a space for herself, she is an International Voice Over Actor with credits in the United States, Europe, Korea & Nigeria lending her craft to PSA's for local and state wide government agencies, commercials, radio ads, telephone IVR's, corporate marketing campaigns and audio books of which she narrates and produce not only her own works but other authors also.

To learn more and book a workshop, visit: www.teworks.org

Otishia Emmens